G000139795

£7.99

A Pillar Box Red Publication

we ♥ love you...

Olly

An Unauthorised 2012 Annual

Written by Maxine Frances Roper
Designed by Sam Macnamara

CONTENTS

3................. We Love You Olly Because

10................. How It All Began

13................. The X Factor

14................. The Xtra Factor

15................. Starfile

16................. Spot The Difference

17................. Discography

18................. Essex Boy

19................. You Know You're An Olly Fan When

21................. Olly Quotes

23................. Olly's Influences

24................. Live On Stage

28................. Olly Quiz

29................. Did You Know?

30................. A - Z of Olly

34................. On This Day

35................. X Factor A History

37................. Olly In The Stars

38................. Famous Friends

42................. Charity Work

43................. Olly Wordsearch

44................. Olly's Ultimate Goal

46................. Hat's The Way I Like It

48................. Olly's Favourite Things

49................. Olly Crossword

50................. Collaborations

52................. Olly Merchandise

53................. Stars On Olly

54................. Olly On Tour Page

56................. Have You Got The Xtra Factor?

58................. Look To The Future

61................. Quiz Answers

we *love* you... Olly

because...

You're a proud Essex boy, and a proud mummy's boy too!

You love your fans, and your trilby hats!

You're a brilliant dancer, and co-write many of your songs

You have a cheeky smile

Your home town has a breakfast named after you

You have top celebrity mates, like JLS and Scouting For Girls

You've done great work for charity, including spending five days in the African desert for Comic Relief

HOW IT ALL BEGAN

From call centre to centre-stage, The X Factor turned Essex Boy Olly Murs into a top-selling pop heartthrob...

Olly was born in Witham, Essex on 14 May 1984. He is of Latvian descent, hence his unusual surname. He is close to his family and he even has a twin brother.

Olly wasn't always destined for pop stardom; his early interests were on the football field. He was a star striker in his school team, and even played semi-professionally for Witham Town FC. But after a torn ligament halted his progress, he became involved in music.

He first sang at his local

pub as part of a duo called Small Town Blaggers with his friend John. Later, while he was working in a call centre for an energy company, his then-girlfriend persuaded him to audition for the X Factor to boost his confidence. It was this audition in 2009 that brought him to public attention. His performance of disco classic

Superstition by Stevie Wonder, was described by judge Simon Cowell as "the easiest 'yes' I've ever given." After coming second to Geordie cutie Joe McElderry in the final, he released his first album, which sold more copies in its first week than any other album in 2010.

The X Factor: From 'Yes' to Success...

Olly's transformation from pub singer to pop idol began on the sixth series of The X Factor in 2009. Performing Stevie Wonder's funk hit Superstition, he became one of the few hundred hopefuls to hear the magic 'Yes' from Simon Cowell and turn their dreams of pop stardom into reality. His trademark style, with cheeky moves and easy grooves, won him an instant following.

With Simon as his mentor, Olly made it through the group stages to the semi-finals, and was the last act of Simon's to remain on the show. His hopes of reaching the final were nearly cut short in Week Seven when he finished in the bottom two with Jedward, after a rendition of George Michael's Fastlove. But he won through, and graced the final with a roof-raising repeat performance of Superstition as well as a moving duet with Robbie Williams featuring Robbie's signature hit Angels. After the show, Robbie is said to have bombarded Olly with invites to his Los Angeles mansion to take part in the charity event Soccer Aid.

Although Olly lost the final vote to Joe McElderry, his place in the X Factor's hall of fame was sealed, and he was immediately offered a record deal with Simon Cowell's label Syco. Hordes of fans turned out in support when he and other finalists toured the country as part of The X Factor Live Tour.

As well as a hit album and sellout tour with fellow X Factor semi-finalists JLS, Olly is due to co-present the eighth series of spinoff show The Xtra Factor with Caroline Flack.

The Xtra Factor

With a top pop career under his belt, Olly has returned to the show that made his name, as presenter of The X Factor spinoff The Xtra Factor, bringing fans exclusive unseen and behind-the scenes footage and gossip from the latest series.

His co-host is Whole 19 Yards and former I'm a Celebrity Get Me Out Of Here presenter Caroline Flack. Caroline once dated Holloways drummer Dave Danger, and was a regular at the Hawley Arms pub in Camden, North London. She claims most celebs don't make crazy dressing room demands anymore, and joked "If I become as big as Cat Deeley I'm going to throw ridiculous diva tantrums!" We're sure Olly takes no 'Flack' from her!

STARFILE

Name: Oliver Stanley Murs

Birthday: 14 May 1984

Born: Witham, Essex

Height: 5'9

Marital Status: Single (and looking!)

Occupation: Singer and Presenter

Ideal Woman: Katie Holmes, Fergie (Black Eyed Peas)

Influences: UB40, Lily Allen, Madness, The Specials, Michael Jackson

Hobbies: Football

Known For: His dance moves, his hats

SPOT THE DIFFERENCE

Olly looks just as gorgeous in both of these pictures but there are 7 differences between them. Can you spot them all?

DISCOGRAPHY

In his short career so far, Olly has scored a hit album, with the highest week one sales for any debut album released in 2010. Olly Murs entered the UK charts at Number Two and went Platinum twice.

Olly Murs

Tracklisting:

1. Change Is Gonna Come
2. Please Don't Let Me Go
3. Thinking Of Me
4. Busy
5. I Blame Hollywood
6. Ask Me To Stay
7. Heart On My Sleeve
8. Hold On
9. Accidental
10. Love Shine Down
11. Don't Say Goodbye
12. A Million More Years

Singles

2010

- Please Don't Let Me Go: Number 1.
- Thinking Of Me: Number 4.
- Heart On My Sleeve: Number 20.
- This One's For The Girls (B Side): Number 69.

2009

- You Are Not Alone (with X Factor finalists): Number 1.

ESSEX BOY

Born and brought up in Witham, Essex, Olly is proud of his Essex roots. Equally proud locals have watched his progress through X Factor on giant screens, turned up in their thousands to see him switch on Christmas lights, and even named a breakfast after him.

ESSEX BOYS
► Work hard and play hard
► Live for the weekend
► Love football, fast cars and girls
► Are all about the banter and jokes
► Always stick up for their mates

FAMOUS ESSEX BOYS
► Gavin and Smithy (Gavin And Stacy)
► Matt Cardle
► Russell Brand
► Dermot O'Leary
► Jamie Oliver
► Jeff Brazier

ESSEX CATCHPHRASES
► "You're 'avin a giggle!"
► "Innit!"
► "Oh my days!"
► "'Ave a word!"
► "Sorted!"
► "Savage!"
► "Oi-Oi!"
► "Know what I mean?"

You Know You're An Olly Fan When...

▶ You sing Superstition in the shower.

▶ ...and imagine Simon Cowell wildly congratulating you afterwards!

▶ You know all the words to Angels because of Olly, not Robbie Williams.

▶ You make a fan video with footage of Olly and Joe McElderry singing The Climb put together so it looks like they're duetting.

▶ You won't go out without a trilby hat on.

▶ You become a huge fan of Manchester United.

▶ Your Facebook news feed has nothing but Olly news...with a bit of JLS news if it mentions Olly!

▶ You decide a funky wiggle-dance is just what your PE lessons need.

▶ You wrap yourself in Christmas paper and present yourself to him at his house (one fan actually did this in 2010!).

▶ You really fancy a trip to Essex.

OLLY QUOTES

When he's not hard at work singing or dancing, Olly's hard at work chatting

On Ambition: "Every artist wants a No 1."

On Songwriting: "It's amazing how you can sit down, and in the space of two or three hours, you can come from a small idea to a really nice song."

On Performing: "We've all had a bad experience on stage, like the stand-up comedian whose gags aren't working. You just learn to go with what works. The first 10 or 15 minutes are the hardest. If that all goes right, they're in the palm of your hand."

On Fans: "I always dreamed of having a fanbase and fans."

On Sport: "I'm a proper football fan, I feel like a bit of a pundit."

On his Music: "I just want to put a smile on the listeners' faces."

On Fashion: "One thing I am really addicted to is buying clothes. I can't help myself."

Olly's Influences

He might be one of a kind, but these pop stars and their music all inspired Olly to pop stardom...

UB40

UB40 were formed in 1978 in Birmingham.

The name 'UB40' comes from a form people used to sign in order to claim unemployment benefit.

They had hits during the 1980s with smoochy reggae-influenced ballads such as Red Red Wine and I Can't Help Falling In Love With You.

The band includes members of English, Scottish, Irish, Yemini and Jamaican heritage.

Lily Allen

Outspoken Lily shot to fame in 2006 with single Smile.

She trained as a florist before she began writing songs.

She is well-known for her use of social networking sites such as MySpace and Twitter.

Like Olly, her songs have mixed pop with reggae.

The Specials

The Specials' music is a mixture of punk and ska.

Their most famous single, Ghost Town, was released in 1981, three years before Olly was born.

Lily Allen and Blur's Damon Albarn are also big fans of the group.

They have reformed twice since splitting in 1984.

Madness

Madness were a ska-pop band from Camden Town, North London.

They hold the record for the most weeks spent by a group in the UK singles chart during the 1980s.

Their hits include Baggy Trousers, Our House and It Must Be Love.

In 2010, they were involved in a charity single project designed to stop the X Factor winner reaching Christmas Number One!

LIVE ON STAGE

Olly faces his adoring fans

Olly couldn't look more
chuffed if he'd just heard
Manchester United had
won a match

Is Olly about to attempt
the moonwalk?

Olly puts his heart and soul into performing

Suits you sir!

A tender moment

Olly Quiz

Test your Olly knowledge with this quick quiz!

1. When is Olly's birthday?

2. What was the name of his first band?

3. Who won The X Factor the year Olly took part?

4. Who originally sang Olly's X Factor audition song?

5. What did Olly do for a living before X Factor?

6. What's the name of the football club he once played for?

7. Who is Olly's ideal woman?

8. Where is the furthest away from home Olly has travelled?

9. What's the name of the B-side to Please Don't Let Me Go, which was written for Olly's female fans?

Answers on Page 61

Did You Know..?

He may have revealed all in a photo shoot but here are some things you might not know about Olly...

♪ Olly attended Notley High School in Essex.

♪ His favourite Michael Jackson song is Billie Jean.

♪ If he was sent to a desert island he would bring a duvet, a pillow, an iPod and a guitar.

♪ Olly describes himself as being addicted to clothes shopping. He wears brands such as Farrah and Fred Perry.

♪ If Olly released a cover single, it would be 'Beautiful' by Akon, sung as a ballad.

♪ He wants to duet with Chris Moyles!

♪ He says if he had to date a member of the same sex it would be David Beckham. "Let's face it, he's pretty good looking!"

♪ Olly went travelling to Australia when he was 20 to improve his confidence.

♪ He claims the longest he was been without a shower is 1-2 weeks. Eeeew!

♪ Olly says he hates being single! Form an orderly queue, girls!

♪ He had never owned a laptop before appearing on X Factor.

♪ Along with T4's Battlefront's Alex Loughlin, Olly broke the Guiness World record for making the most cups of tea in an hour, with a staggering 496 brews!

♪ Olly has a birthmark in an unusual place he doesn't want to reveal!

♪ Olly once appeared on Deal Or No Deal, and won £10.

A-Z of OLLY

A: is for Acting: Olly has always fancied a part in EastEnders and even said he'd have a fling with grandma Dot Cotton to get onto the show!

B: is for Brit Awards: Olly was nominated for Best Single for Please Don't Let Me Go in 2011.

C: is for Charity: Olly combines fame and a love of football to help good causes like Soccer Relief and Manchester United Relief.

D: is for Dance moves: The 'Olly wiggle' helped to define The X Factor in 2009, and Olly says he holds dance-offs on nights out!

E: is for Essex: Essex boy Olly began singing in his local pub. Proud locals watched his X Factor success on big screens around the town.

F: is for Football: Olly loves to play and watch the game, especially Manchester United.

G: is for Gorgeous: Amazingly, Olly doesn't think he is! "But if girls think I'm hot, that's great!" he adds.

H: is for Hats: Stylish Olly's hat collection is ever-growing and he says it's because he's lazy about doing his hair. His gran has even knitted some of them!

I: is for Indie Rock: Along with reggae, this is Olly's favourite kind of music. With pop and hip-hop acts storming the summer festivals, perhaps an Olly Murs set at Glastonbury isn't far off!

J: is for Joe McElderry: Joe pipped Olly to the post to win X Factor. Good sport Olly admitted he was "gutted" to have lost X Factor but backed Joe's bid for the Christmas Number One.

K: is for Katie Holmes: Watch out Tom Cruise, Olly admits to having a crush on the ex-Dawson's Creek star.

L: is for Lativa: Olly is part Latvian. Latvia's biggest pop star, Lauris Reiniks, has released seven solo albums since 1998. In 2010, his single "Es skrienu" ("I Will Run") was translated into five languages.

M: is for Manchester United: He might be an Essex boy but when it comes to football, his heart's in Old Trafford.

A-Z of OLLY

N: is for Normal Guy: Despite his fame, Olly says his feet are firmly on the ground: "I don't expect to be a massive superstar with everyone knowing who I am," he says.

O: is for Other Half: Happily for his female fans, Olly doesn't have one! He's currently single.

P: is for Please Don't Let Me Go: Olly's debut single is about a girl who dumped him out of the blue just as they were getting serious. Awww!

Q: is for Quality: He might be cheeky and chilled, but Olly insists he isn't just a cheesy pop star and wants his music to be taken seriously.

R: is for Robbie Williams: Olly counts Robbie as one of his best mates after they duetted on X Factor.

S: is for Small Town Blaggers: This is the name of the pub duo Olly sang in with his best friend before hitting the bigtime.

T: is for Thank Yous: Olly was so chuffed by one fan, who gifted him a personalised Manchester United shirt, that he gave her a ticket to his show as a thank you!

U: is for UB40: The 80s reggae band who had hits such as I Can't Help Falling In Love With You are among Olly's influences.

V: is for Vicky-Lynn Murs aka Olly's mum: She sometimes answers her mummy's-boy son's fan mail. Her maiden name is Vicky Pollard!

W: is for Who Wants To Be A Millionaire?: Olly proved he's not just a pretty face when he won £10,000 for charity on the show's celebrity version.

X: is for X-Rated: Cheeky Olly made a bet that he would pose naked for Heat Magazine if Please Don't Let Me Go made it to number one. It did, and he did! Swoon!

Y: is for Young Summers: Olly spent most of his childhood summers playing football with his twin brother, and as a passenger in his uncle's lorry.

Z: is for Zzzz: One thing we're sure busy Olly doesn't do much of these days!

On This Day...

Olly entered the world on 14 May 1984, along with his twin brother. But what else happened on that very special day? Find out here:

- Olly shares his birthday with 80s music legend David Byrne from Talking Heads, Natalie Appleton from 90s girl band All Saints, and actresses Cate Blanchett and Martine McCutcheon.

- The Number One UK single was Reflex by New Romantic legends Duran Duran.

  The Number One UK album was Legend: The Best of Bob Marley & The Wailers.

- An estimated 20,000 miners and their wives from Yorkshire, Scotland and South Wales took part in a protest march during the miner's strike.

- King of Pop Michael Jackson was presented with a Humanitarian Award by US President Ronald Reagan.

The X Factor A History

The story of the show that made Olly a star

It's hard to ever imagine Saturday nights without it, but The X Factor began in the UK back in 2004. After the success of Pop Idol, which made stars of the likes of Will Young and Gareth Gates, judge Simon Cowell wanted his own show, and X Factor became its replacement.

Over 50,000 people auditioned for the first series. Judged by Simon, along with Sharon Osborne and Louis Walsh, it was won by Steve Brookstein. But it was the success of superstars Shayne Ward and Leona Lewis in 2005 and 2006 that made the show into a phenomenon, attracting over 19.7 million viewers and 200,000 auditions, with 10 million people voting in the final.

Since the show began, a number of changes have been made to the format. For example, the audition stages now take place in front of an audience, instead of just the judges, and, for some lucky contestants, the judge's boot camps take place abroad. Olly found out he was through to the final while in LA, which he described as one of the best experiences of his life.

All seven winners of X Factor have had their first singles reach Number One in the charts, either at Christmas or New Year.

X Factor Winners & Runners Up 2004-2010

► 2004 Steve Brookstein (Runner Up: G4)

► 2005 Shayne Ward (Runner Up: Andy Abraham)

► 2006 Leona Lewis (Runner Up: Ray Quinn)

► 2007 Leon Jackson (Runner Up: Rhydian Roberts)

► 2008 Alexandra Burke (Runner: Up JLS)

► 2009 Joe McElderry (Runner Up: Olly Murs)

► 2010 Matt Cardle (Runner Up: Rebecca Ferguson)

Did You Know..?

• The show is currently set to run until 2013

• X Factor-themed goodies have included clothes, jewellery, make-up and even pizzas!

Olly In The Stars

What's Olly like? Could you win Olly's heart? Find out with this handy guide to Olly's star sign

Olly was born on 14 May 1984, making him a Taurus

Taurus Traits:

- Patient and reliable
- Warm-hearted and loving
- Persistent and determined
- Placid and security loving
- Love the outdoors

Taurus Troubles

- Taurans can be jealous or possessive
- Taurans hate being rushed
- Taurans love quality, and have expensive tastes

Top Love Matches

- Capricorn
- Virgo
- Scorpio

37

Olly is a firm favourite among X Factor contestants and the pop and football A List.

ROBBIE WILLIAMS

Olly became good mates with Robbie after their duet during the X Factor final.

Robbie has sold more than 57 million albums worldwide, and he holds the world record for the most concert tickets sold in one day.

He won the 2010 Brit Award for Outstanding Contribution to British Music.

JLS

Britain's biggest boyband have toured with Olly.

Before his naked photoshoot with Heat magazine, he asked for their advice on how to look good naked!

FRIENDS

These are some of his celebrity pals and inspirations:

FOOTALL GREATS

Manchester United's Wayne Rooney is Olly's favourite player.

Olly has rubbed shoulders with football stars such as Jamie Redknapp and Teddy Sheringham during his charity work for Soccer Aid and Manchester United Relief.

THE X FACTOR GANG

Olly still keeps in touch with Joe, Dan, Jamie and Lloyd, saying: "We shared one of the most amazing experiences you can have."

His top mate is fellow Essex resident Stacey Solomon.

Charity Work

Caring Olly is proud of his work for charity. As well as teaming up for X Factor charity singles, he has supported a few good causes of his own...

SOCCER RELIEF

In June 2010 Olly took part in Soccer Relief. The event, which was held at Manchester United's ground Old Trafford, featured celebrities and footballers from across the world playing the beautiful game to raise money for charity. The England Team was captained by Olly's mate and lifelong Port Vale fan Robbie Williams. Sadly, the Rest of the World team won after a goal from Hollywood actor Woody Harrelson, but the England Team put up a good fight. It wasn't just the football entertaining the crowds - Heat magazine captured Olly pulling some very funny grimaces indeed!

COMIC RELIEF

Olly faced a challenge greater than Simon Cowell when he

signed up to the BT Charity Trek as part of the 2011 Comic Relief Red Nose Day campaign. He and other celebrities, including Kara Tointon,

Dermot O'Leary and Lorraine Kelly, spent five days in the Kaisut desert in North Kenya, covering 100km (62 miles) in temperatures of up to 40 degrees Celsius. The group raised around 1.4 million pounds. "It was one of the best things I've ever done," he says.

MAKE A WISH FOUNDATION

Olly has met fans on behalf of the Make A Wish Foundation, which grants wishes to seriously ill children. In July 2011, he met four year-old devoted fan Mia-Jade, who suffers from a rare condition called Septo-Optic Dysplasia, making her blind, and he gave her one of his famous hats! Mia-Jade's mother said: "She's over the moon. She talks about the wish non-stop and his hat is hanging in her room now!"

OLLY ON CHARITY WORK:

"It's probably the best thing about being famous and being given this opportunity. You are able to help and support other people and make a difference."

Olly Wordsearch

Can you find the Olly related words?

ANGELS	JLS	TAURUS
ESSEX	LATVIAN	TRILBY
FOOTBALL	REGGAE	TWIN

```
V  F  W  Y  R  O  T  C  A  F  X
T  P  O  R  B  H  N  X  L  T  D
V  D  G  O  W  L  E  R  M  D  T
P  V  V  V  T  S  I  R  T  N  L
R  N  Q  L  S  B  E  R  F  I  V
G  A  F  E  R  G  A  S  T  W  L
M  N  Y  K  G  Q  U  L  M  T  T
F  G  M  A  N  R  H  M  L  Y  S
R  E  E  B  U  T  F  V  L  M  L
C  L  L  A  T  V  I  A  N  N  J
K  S  T  R  K  D  M  L  D  J  T
```

Olly's Ultimate Goal

Before singing, it was football that captured Olly's heart. The Manchester United supporter went from star school striker to playing semi-professionally for Essex's Witham Town FC. His PE teacher admits that he wasn't known for singing football songs or having unique goal celebrations. But Olly's X Factor triumph has also brought him closer to his footballing heroes.

In 2010, Olly played football for United Relief Live: The Big Red Family Day Out, a bank holiday charity extravaganza hosted by Manchester United at their Old Trafford ground to raise money for Sport Relief and local development projects. The match, featuring a mix of stars and club legends, was coached by the club's first-team coach Rene Meulensteen.

Olly said: "I'm so excited to walk out through the tunnel at Old Trafford. I've been an avid Manchester United fan all my life and so the experience will simply be up there as one of the best moments in my life so far. My fellow team-mate Dwight Yorke was here today showing off a few skills – I'm pleased that I'm on his side!"

Hat's The Way I Like It!

Olly's known for his sense of style, especially for his hats. Check out these snaps of Olly sporting a range of headgear....

OLLY ON FASHION:

"All my mates say, 'You're like a woman', and I tell them, 'Yeah, but I just like looking good."

Olly's Favourite Things:

BAND: UB40

SINGER: Michael Jackson

FOOTBALL TEAM: Manchester United

DRINK: Tea

COLOUR: Blue

X FACTOR CRUSH: Cheryl Cole

LUXURY ITEM: A £1000 Dior coat

SUPERPOWER: X Ray vision

Olly Crossword

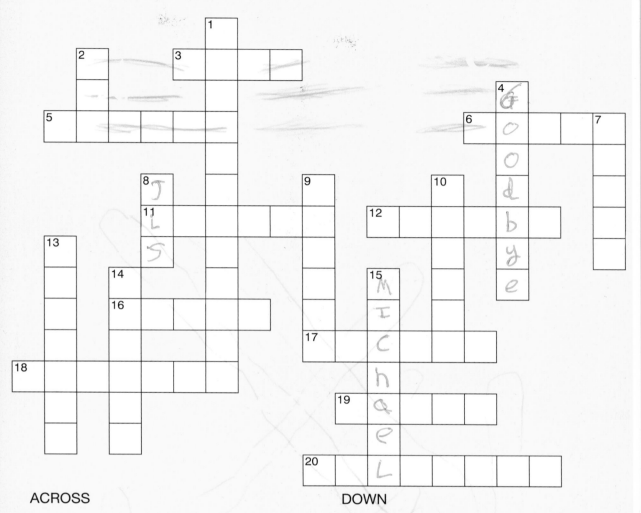

Grid handwritten entries:
- 8 Down: J L S
- 4 Down: G O O D B Y E
- 15 Down: M I C H A E L
- 20 Across (first letter): L

ACROSS

3 A song title that could describe Olly's life! (4)

5 Matt _____. Fellow Essex boy and X Factor star (6)

6 Olly's mates call him this because of his passion for fashion (5)

11 Country Olly's surname (and his dad's family) comes from (6)

12 Type of hat Olly often wears (6)

16 Olly's favourite kind of music (5)

17 _____ Aid. Football charity Olly likes to support (6)

18 Olly claims this is his only addiction (7)

19 First name of Olly's favourite Manchester United player (5)

20 Robbie _____. Olly's mate and duet partner in the X Factor final (8)

DOWN

1 Song Olly sang during his first X Factor audition (12)

2 Olly set a record for drinking this (3)

4 Don't Say _____. Song title. (7)

7 Type of photoshoot Olly did when Please Don't Let Me Go reached Number One (5)

8 Boy band Olly toured with (3)

9 Olly's star sign (6)

10 What Olly likes to do with his hips (6)

13 Vicky _____. Little Britain character Olly's mum shares her maiden name with (7)

14 Town in Essex where Olly hails from (6)

15 _____ Jackson - this King of Pop is Olly's idol (7)

Collaborations

During The X Factor, and beyond Olly has collaborated with an exciting range of other artists and songwriters. He was reported to be working with Professor Green on the single Thinking Of Me. Unfortunately this fell through at the last minute. Stars he'd like to collaborate with include Akon, Paolo Nutini and Chris Moyles!

► Robbie Williams – Angels (X Factor final duet)

► X Factor Live

► Future Cut

► Scouting For Girls

► Trevor Horn

► Rizzle Kicks

Scouting For Girls

Akon

Paulo Nutini

Trevor Horn

Professor Green

Olly Merchandise

Get your Olly fix around the web and in your pocket with a range of Olly merchandise

Olly on Facebook: facebook.com/ollymurs

Olly On Twitter: twitter.com/ollyofficial

Olly's Official Website:

http://www.olly-murs-music.com/

Olly's official website features a range of approved merchandise, including:

I Love Olly Murs t-shirt

I Love Olly Murs girls' skinny tee

I Love Olly Murs keyring

I Love Olly Murs wristband

Stars on Olly....

What others have been saying about Olly:

"The easiest 'yes' I've ever given" - Simon Cowell

"He's the dark horse; the one to watch"
- Louis Walsh

"Olly likes to strip off every now and then. We'd be waiting outside to go on stage and his dressing room might be next to the stage and he'd come out and be in his boxers!"
- Jodi Albert (Wonderland)

Have You Got The

Xtra Factor?

Try this fun quiz to see if you could follow in Olly's footsteps

1. Your crush is walking down the corridor but your hair's a mess! Do you:

a) Belt out your best Leona impression at him
b) Apologise for your hair and ask about Friday night's party
c) Hide behind a locker until he goes away

2. What would you do to become a pop star?

a) Work in a call centre, singing to entertain your colleagues
b) Study hard and sing in the school concert
c) Flip burgers in McDonalds, hoping your favourite celeb will drop in!

3. What's your best chat-up line?

a) "Wanna hear my version of The Climb?"
b) "You could be on The X Factor!"
c) "Fancy some chips?"

4. What's your idea of a typical night out?

a) Hours of karaoke
b) An evening in front of The X Factor with takeaway
c) An evening playing Angry Birds on your phone

5. What makes a great pop star?

a) A great singing voice
b) Bags of personality
c) Getting back at your mum for giving your pet rabbit away when you were 8

6. You audition for X Factor and Simon says you're not quite there yet. What do you do?

a) Save the date for next year's audition
b) Bawl your eyes out
c) Photoshop devil horns onto a picture of Simon and save it as your phone's wallpaper

Mostly As': You've definitely got it! Keep going and you could be ogling Olly at the next X Factor wrap party.
Mostly Bs': You're definitely a contender. Practice with that hairbrush mike and you'll get there soon.
Mostly Cs': Oh dear! Don't start practising your autograph just yet.

Look To The Future

He set the pop world alight in 2011. What does the future hold for Olly?

- LOVE: Olly has been romantically linked to a string of stars from the Wonderland girls to the cast of The Only Way Is Essex. Will any of the rumours prove to be true?

- FLYING THE NEST: Olly has recently moved out of his parents' pad in Essex and is looking at pads in London's trendy Camden and Shoreditch.

- MUSIC: His second studio album is set to be the soundtrack to 2012.

- COLLABORATIONS: Will his summer tour with JLS lead to a hot new joint single?

- FASHION: Olly recently said he's stopped wearing his hats because everyone comments on it. Will style slave Olly have a new fashion trademark soon?

JLS

Wonderland girls

The Only Way is Essex

QUIZ ANSWERS

Page 28

1. 14th May
2. Small Town Blaggers
3. Joe McElderry
4. Stevie Wonder
5. Call centre worker
6. Witham Town FC
7. Katie Holmes
8. Australia
9. One For The Girls

Page 16

Page 43

Page 49